Seeking Signs, Finding Wonders

Vivian Kearney

The opinions expressed in this book are solely the opinions of the author and do not represent the opinions or thoughts of the publisher. The author has represented and warranted full ownership and/or legal right to publish all the materials in this book.

Seeking Signs, Finding Wonders
All Rights Reserved
Copyright © 2014, Vivian Kearney
Cover illustration © 2014, Vivian Kearney –All rights reserved, used with permission
Pukiyari Publishers

This book may not be reproduced, transmitted, or stored in whole or in part by any means, including graphic, electronic, or mechanical without the express written consent of the author, except in the case of brief quotations embodied in critical articles and reviews.

ISBN-10: 163065020X
ISBN-13: 978-1-63065-020-9

PRINTED IN THE UNITED STATES OF AMERICA
www.pukiyari.com

*Dedicated to my beloved husband, Milo,
our children, grandchildren and families.*

And to the preservation of this grace-given planet.

Table of Contents

Quest 11
- Seeking Signs 12
- Treasure Hunt 13
- Jewelled Sands 14

Clues, Moods and Marvels 15
- Just Because 16
- Clues 17
- Rain in Montreal 18
- Twilight in San Antonio 19
- Retreat - 2013 20
- January Reverie 21
- One Day 22
- Reed in the Wind 23
- Baby Cenizo 24
- Dancing Art 25

Nature Speaks 27
- Dawn 28
- Workout 29
- Sympathy All Around 30
- Singing Trees 31
- Activist Trees 32
- Trees as Poets 33
- Critics Everywhere 34
- Bee-Attitudes 35
- Wildflower Competition 36
- Spectators 37
- Black Friday Commentaries 38
- Neighborhood Crossing 39
- Vigilance Haiku 40
- Bookstore Readings 41
- Surprized 42

Newsworthy Turtle 43
Trick or Treat 44
The Stone's Song 45

Authorized 47
Commissioned 48
Healing Birds 49
The Flower Cure 50
What's Good About Dust 51
Forgiveness 52
Algae Versus Civilization 53
Trying to Help 54
Snake in the Grass 55

Relating to Nature 57
Franciscan Relatives 58
Mandalas 59
At the LBJ Texas White House 60
Padre Island 61
Scobee Planetarium 62
Personification Meditation 63
Stewardship or Dominion? 64
Good Intentions 65
Couldn't We Get Along? 66
Suggested Application 67
Story of a Family Pet 68
Magazine Information 70

The Earth Travails 71
Many Hopeful Rainbows 72
Revisiting Merlin 73
Flattened 74
Deconstruction 75
On the Way Out 76
Sentinels 77

Oiled 78
Yellowstone Lake 79

Seasonal 81
Meditating Season 82
Autumn Moon 83
Late Fall 84
Winter From Above 85
Montreal Winter 86
San Antonio in Winter 87
Spring Power Points 88
Spring in San Antonio 89
Our Street Awakens 90
Ice-Cream Summer 91
Summer in the Rio Grande Valley 92
Watering the Sunset 93

Whither the Weather 95
Global Warming 96
Northern Memories 97
Drought - 2010 98
Drought - 2011 99
Dry News 100
Drought - 2012 101
Possible Sign - 2013 102
Summer - 2014 103
Torn the Feathers 104
Documentary - Sunken Paradise 105
Concerns 106
Tearing the Bonds 107

Save Us (Hoshianu) 109
Across Time 110
Lost 111
They Will Start to Sing 112

Holy Ground 113
Wellsprings Chapel 114
At the Bench 115
Prismatic 116

Quest

Vivian Kearney

Seeking Signs

What tangible signs do we seek?
For what reassurance?
What answering wonders wander around us
Mostly unseen and unheard
From a parallel, peaceful world?

Treasure Hunt

Searching for the pink,
The pink of love
Searching for the green,
The green of life
Searching for the blue,
The blue of answers
Searching for the brown,
The brown of security,
Searching for the purple,
The purple of creativity,
Searching for the gold
The gold of knowledge
Searching for the red,
The red of energy,
Searching for the orange,
The orange of happiness
Searching for the yellow,
The yellow of hope

While
A rainbow smile
Points to treasures
From the sky

Vivian Kearney

Jewelled Sands

We
Grind down the diamonds
Of God's miracles
Into fine sand
On humdrum shores

Then we wait for more
Signs and wonders
To float
From the horizon

Not realizing
That we stand
On mines of incredible jewels
Wrought by His hand

Clues, Moods and Marvels

Vivian Kearney

Just Because

Just because
An ethereal dawn
Hovers over
A four-leaf clover
Reviving our wishes
For good luck
Signs and wonders

Then evaporates
As the dew
Into the day's busy
Commonalities

Doesn't mean
That the marvel-planting God
Didn't just
Talk to us

Clues

Every tree whispers, all the birds sing
Clouds write that above everything
We are each called to do good works
In deeds, thoughts, prayers and words

The intricate patterns around us, inside
The grasses sprouting in deserts too wide
The moments when poems give moods a voice
For all these graces, Lord, let us rejoice

Vivian Kearney

Rain in Montreal

The rain pours
The trees moan and dance
Seeming possessed
By something beyond

The rain pours
And near the lamplights
Droplets turn to diamonds
And dance for joy

The rain pours
And a strange grey color
Lights the skies
And washes the ground

The rain pours
While my soul
Walks the city streets
To sing with the trees

Twilight in San Antonio

Right after the rain
In the purple-blue twilight
Out of newly lush deep green grass
Three bright white day lilies
Near our pale turquoise fountain
Shine

Like three sparkling stars
Recently fallen
From cloudy skies
Promising enchanted
Lullabies

Vivian Kearney

Retreat - 2013

Lovely the sunset in the hill country
Seen through one great oak tree's
Intricately curved branches

Quiet our time for writing exercises
Are the trees writing also?
With the clouds as their notebooks

Calm this meditating evening
Diving down, down, down for
Our voices under the blue mountains

Our souls looking to the
Farewell twilight sky

January Reverie

Glass fragile the afternoon light
And hushed the white blinds as I write
About evolving blues outside

That create moveable paintings
Lines and angles
On the waiting walls and furniture

Placid things that patiently
Await reorganization
For a renewing year

Soothing the world of trees, bushes, grasses
Of the yard outside, portraited
Through cool windows
That frame the slopes
Of neighboring roofs

Space becomes timeless
Schedules stop for the day
Until the train restarts

Vivian Kearney

One Day

The just dreamed tune skipped gladly,
Hummed merrily in my mind,
Then just as jovially, carelessly,
Left and danced out again

The clouds sailed solemnly
Calmly, kaleidescopically by
And the day's eight track tape
Miraculously restarted its loop.

The waves of my moods
Ebbed and flowed laboriously
With the ship of faith sometimes
Hard to see in the distance

The sun set amazingly quickly,
Descending rapidly on the horizon
Like a neon peach basketball
Aimed at a hidden holding net

Ambulance sirens in the night
Trailing dog barks like ribbons
Only star points of light now in the sky
But their diamonds spell out hope

Reed in the Wind

The reed
Is a lovely thing
With every gust of wind
It bends to caress the waters
Sighs its thankfulness to eternity
And celebrates it with a dance
Of slow-mounting frenzy
The reed
Is a lovely thing

Vivian Kearney

Baby Cenizo

Baby Cinderella plant —
Tiny sagebrush in our yard
Is also flowering
Bravely along with its older relatives
On far hills and near streets
For this appointed
Purpling time

Dancing Art

Watercolor sky
Featherpainted trees
Crayoned clouds
Penciled green grass

India ink cats
Oil-painted sun
Charcoal birds
Pastel flowers

All dancing, swaying
To unheard
Cosmic music

Vivian Kearney

Nature Speaks

Vivian Kearney

Dawn

All His moments are
A deepening teaching
Said the dawn-opening sky
As it solemnly
Moved through its stages
Of
Understanding night purple
Majestic dark hues
Onward through a spiritual
Pale new blue
Day

Workout

As I wake up and wisely
Start exercising
The brightening sky
Jauntily says —
Watch me
Do my color workout

Vivian Kearney

Sympathy All Around

Look at us, listen to us
Sighing with you

A tearful grey sky
Gently nodding branches
The sun streaming encouragement
A slivery moon
Flashing a knowing silver smile
The stillness is no longer silent

We too are suffering
With Jesus on the cross
Of the world's tragedies

Singing Trees

Listen —
Each tree
Whether feathered delicately
With narrow pale green spring leaves
Or fringed with lacy white blooms
Or painted with flaming colors
Its grainy trunk monochrome
Or birch paper delicate
Or cedar bark peeling nervously

Sings a different song
In a major or minor key
But none
Discordant or wrong

Vivian Kearney

Activist Trees

The trees demonstrate too
Waving their placard leaves
Supportively
Murmuring — we can help
Your greening concerns
Exchanging oxygen for your carbon dioxide
Offering beauty, shade, restful vistas —

Please don't cut us down
Except for some good causes
And helpful signs

Trees as Poets

If a tree could write
A poem with its delicate branches
Using the sky as dappled paper

Would it be a prayer
That people
Our omnivorous species

Could recognize
Protect and cherish
Its still gifts
Of beautiful comfort

Vivian Kearney

Critics Everywhere

Here, let me help you
Photosynthesize
Said the vine
As it wrapped and leafed
Around a telephone pole
Chiding its
Unbranching role

Nature Speaks

Bee-Attitudes

Gathering the nectar of metaphors
From our symbol-laden thoughts
Let's make honey, o sweet honey
Of nourishing, gladdening poetry

Vivian Kearney

Wildflower Competition

This field is our domain
Waved the snow-drop weeds
Gracefully

While fiesta-colored blooms
On the other side
Of the hurrying street

Vied for the memory prize
Of our fleeting eyes

Spectators

Bird-like cameras perched on lamps
What do they twitter about the drivers below?
Camera-like birds punctuating wires
Sharing news about their sky empires

Vivian Kearney

Black Friday Commentaries

A shimmering blue-black grackle
Strolls philosophically
Down the morning sidewalk
Crackling to itself
Some stoical statements

While I get today's paper
Advertising extraordinary deals
And hear the radio
Delivering non-ending commentaries
In our special language

Neighborhood Crossing

Proud, plump, self-assured
Maybe a household's pet
A strange beige peacock
Wants to cross the road

We barely miss it
Musing it may be
In need of other bird mentors
Or maybe stricter structures

It signals —
Slow down
Watch where you're going
You're trespassing

Vivian Kearney

Vigilance Haiku

Sorry, neighbor dog
Barking worriedly about
My insomniac lights

Bookstore Readings

On the pet care shelf
Eight, no twenty
Friendly dog's eyes
On book covers
Empathetically
Listen to our feelings
At our poetry readings

Vivian Kearney

Surprized

Dear deer in the headlights
Surprized out of your borrowed domain
Wondering why your mild wildness
Brought this fearsome lonely brightness

Nature Speaks

Newsworthy Turtle

What
Do you expect from me?
Thought the green sea turtle
With its bulging extra-terrestrial eyes
I've been caught in a weather change
I can't smile or wave
Why bother to hold me
To take a survivor's newspaper picture
For your breakfast table?

Vivian Kearney

Trick or Treat

Feral
Cats go out Halloweening
Every day, every night
With their glittery eyes
Twitching whiskers
Stealthy fur, yawling —

You know those sweet little birds —
Cardinals, bluebirds
Even little sparrows
You love to watch

I will trick them and eat them
And leave their feathers on your lawn
If you don't give me some
Tasty treat

The Stone's Song

The stone's song
Hums deep within
Its eon layers
In harmony with
The aged mountains'
Bass voices
In the choir
Of creation

Vivian Kearney

Authorized

Vivian Kearney

Commissioned

The business of flowers is...
Advertising
With patterns, shapes,
Colors

The theme of flowers is...
Sweetness
To make bees
Buzz with joy

The mission of flowers is...
Contributing
To ecosystems
Wisely

The message of flowers is...
God's creativity —
Inventive,
Lovely

Authorized

Healing Birds

Across the windows
Of our pain
Flies a happily colored bird
Refreshed by
Chanced or blessed
Sparkling rain

Vivian Kearney

The Flower Cure

A single flower
Talks about the sun
And the rain
And we
Are restored

Authorized

What's Good About Dust

A little dust
Protects the furniture
A few germs
Offer antibodies
Less gifts
Do more

Unfair —
No, blessing
Stifling —
No, cozy
Unjust —
No, merciful
Unforeseen...
Yes, grace

Glass half empty —
No, enough
Fatalistic knots
No, misunderstood carpet
For His footsteps
On the patterns
Of my life

Vivian Kearney

Forgiveness

Paper trash dancing around us
Plastic bags flapping above us
But as we grow, glow in all colors
We forgive you with our beauty

Authorized

Algae Versus Civilization

Miniscule green algae
Conglomerated
Into bigger splotches

Did you want to
Were you meant to

Create naturalistic
Unpredictable designs

Blurring the squared geometry
Of the swimming pool's
Tan tiles symmetry

Vivian Kearney

Trying to Help

Flowers try
So beautifully
Quietly and sweetly
With their pinks and blues
Purples, whites and yellows
Reds and oranges
To make us smile

Snake in the Grass

Feel sorry for the slithering snake
Everybody hates it
Nobody loves it
As it slinks around
On the sheltering cool ground

Feel sorry for its victims
As it bites their Achilles' heel
One day it will be captured
Sent to a science lab
For the good of its predator

Vivian Kearney

Relating to Nature

Vivian Kearney

Franciscan Relatives

Draw it,
Pin it down —
Understand its veins
Recreate the structures
Breathe alongside
Your brothers, the trees
Your sisters, the flowers
All nature with the same
Mega heart
Wavelength
Electro-magnetic
Resonance
As you

Mandalas

The sun
The moon
Flowers, planets and stars
Are mandalas
Entreating us
Teaching us
To glow for God
Also

Vivian Kearney

At the LBJ Texas White House

Painting broadly blocked
With greys and greyish greens
A lady in a red dress
Black bouffant hair
Waving at the sky —
Lady Bird?
Thanking the heavens
For watering her Texas
Wildflowers

Padre Island

Smiling, the sandy children
Dressed formally, the seagulls,
Colorful, the mushrooming umbrellas,
Jovial, the beachwalkers going back home
After communing
With God's billowing
Reminder of creation

Vivian Kearney

Scobee Planetarium

Things did work out
Serendipitously
Or was it miraculously?

Who tossed this beautiful
Marbled earth into this twirling
Galaxy and, as a generous king,
Gave it just the right clouds?

Other planets now pasted so prettily
On our telescoped eyes gravely wander
Do they know we observe them in wonder
Trying to quantify their lives

From our cozy, domed planetarium
As do other peoples, as did the ancients
Seeking answers, asking to be sent
Keys to this echoing universe

Personification Meditation

Do birds' hearts burst with happiness
As they flutter from tree to tree
Enjoying their acrobatic swirls
Do birds feel gratefulness?

Do trees feel proud
As they grow towards the sky
Leaves dancing in the winds
Conversing with the clouds?

Do grasses feel humbly smug
Humming green melodies
Redeeming cold cement
With tufts of living rugs?

Do flowers love flaunting
Their colorful, perfumed clothes
And shouldn't we also celebrate
With our siblings wonderful?

Vivian Kearney

Stewardship or Dominion?

With all the getting, hoarding
Why are we so forlorn?
Feeling nature's scorn?

Could it be because we've lost the seas
Birds, animals, flowers, skies, trees, bees
Marking most for destruction
With one word's mistranslation?

Good Intentions

Here, let me protect you
Said man to the planet's flora and fauna
I'll create special parks, nature reservations

But the sheep clothing is tattered
To evidence rapacious
Wolf teeth
That gobble wildlife and wildlands
By the second

Vivian Kearney

Couldn't We Get Along?

Couldn't we have industrialized without a revolution
Against nature
Couldn't we stop torturing animals and
Still find needed cures
Couldn't we write and dwell without killing
So many trees
Couldn't we live and let live
In loving charity?

Suggested Application

Listen to the birds
Speaking to the eyes of your heart
But we don't
We cut them, shoot them
Down
For they don't count
In our time-bound patterns
Our pavemented
Arrangements

Maybe if they could
Maybe if we would
Develop an app
We would have the technology
To communicate with their wonders

Vivian Kearney

Story of a Family Pet

Farming, gardening
Had I none
Planting, tending
All not done
With my big cities background

But later we had some pets
Flanvie was one dog's name
(Flanbhui to be Irish exact)
Belonging to our son

An orange clad gentleman of a Pomeranian
Though in his youth mischievous
About running anywhere
Down the neighborhood's
Inviting sidewalks

But his emotions grew up abruptly
When one day his disappearing pranks
Persuaded his best friend forever,
Our daughter's Shih Tzu,
To running too

Relating to Nature

That little Shih Tzu never came back
And Flanvie was so sorry
He put his head on my lap
Sighing
And never explored
Those lovely other lawns
On his own again

He stayed close,
Loved to have his fur rubbed,
Walking to McDonald's and Dairy Queen
(On a leash)
And shared his food
With any bird, mouse, cat, possum
That came along

Finally, old and very sick
He gave us a long sweet look
And a tired sigh
As he was put to sleep
His head on our laps
And we cried

Vivian Kearney

Magazine Information

Anything more touching
Than a care giraffe soothing
A man dying
From cancer

Anything more funny
Than a dog deciding to walk
Its plush toys in a stroller
Imitatively

Anything more beautiful
Than amazing friendships
Communications among species
Deeper than symbiosis

Anything more vulnerable
Than our amicable Holocene era
Rapidly become Anthropocene
Succeeding to the point of failure

The Earth Travails

Vivian Kearney

Many Hopeful Rainbows

Billions of individual rainbows —
The world's population in fact —
Each representing personal plans, stories,
Hopes, skills, wills, beauty, memory

All awaiting
God's tears and smiles arc
Encompassing this so far
Badly stewarded earth,
Our homeland

Revisiting Merlin

We have gone so far, so very far
In our searches over the oceans
Of reality, influenced by our dreams
And subliminal proclivities

Way into developing predictable
Cities with many right-angled
Scientific discoveries about how
The universe really moves

And works — but alack and alas
Our groves have been cut down
Deer runs are now new suburbs

Is Merlin, the shapechanger
Proud of our clever alchemy?

Vivian Kearney

Flattened

Silhouette leaping on the yellow road sign
The shadow of a deer gives us
A sense of oneness with nature
A feeling it's still around
Though two-dimensionally
Flattened

Oak Kingdom city division,
Its name a rear view mirror for our culture,
Evoking a never-again land
Has used up all its trees
For our boxy dwellings

Lake Vista district has no lake
Even some mountains are gone
What have we wrought and wrestled?
What have we won?

Deconstruction

We designate
Those yellow/orange/white
Trunk bands…
Arm bands…
To stay in step
With progression's
Cleansing commands

O trees
O souls
Let us say
Prayers and *kaddish*
For you
For us
The melancholy
Temporary
Survivors

Vivian Kearney

On the Way Out

What happened to our beautiful cold habitat?
Roared the remaining polar bears disconsolately
We camouflaged, adapted, built communities
Now we have no idea where anything's at

Whales following their dead inexorably
Mourning their lost brethren tragically
We tried to beat them back to reviving seas
But now our human friendship failed miserably

Sentinels

The leafy rows of trees
Lining the highways
So tamed, so patronized
Their life-relaying existence
Allowed a few more weeks, years
Until they are felled
For and by
More carbon

Though they reassume
Some of their mystery, dignity
At night
As noble savages
Dark sentinels
Miraging a previously
Organic planet

Vivian Kearney

Oiled

Electricity purrs
In our houses, on the streets
Through the air, buildings, cars

As a contented, sated cat
Lapping the earth's wealth

Until it becomes
A roaring lion
Devouring, consuming us

In the gulf
Of our desires

Yellowstone Lake

Listen,
From the depths
Of this lost planet
The lake is singing...

No —
It's crying

Vivian Kearney

Seasonal

Vivian Kearney

Meditating Season

It's like
Meditating under
A mystical tree

Maybe not
As much as I could be
Doing

I gather leaves,
Yellow, red, orange
And weave them into lines

Maybe rhymed, alliterated
Into fun to write
Woven poetry

Then those patterned cloths
Can be arranged
Into quilted blankets

To portray autumn's
Colorfully aging
And dying season

Seasonal

Autumn Moon

Autumn moon shining bright
You seem to be frowning
Are we such a sad sight

Are you chiding us for earth's blight
Against our pollution travailling
Surpassing even warnings erudite

May we soon expedite
Solutions to our blind destroying
Before our autumn becomes night

Vivian Kearney

Late Fall

The trembling golden leaves
Tired of being paintbrush strokes
Against the steel-grey sky
Cry as they fall
On the wintry ground

Just so
God weeps with every loss
Sharing each burden from the cross

Winter From Above

In the land of the clouds
You can hike through woolly mountains,
See back-lit lagoons, fairy castles
And dragon rivers snaking below

Bright blue skies
Are presented as portraits
Inside puffy grey frames

With its grey and white
Blocked patches
The partially frozen ground
Looks like
A soccer ball
Laid flat and low

Ice brackets
The still flowing
Nearing river

How indescribably beautiful
In any metaphorical language
The earth speaks through the sadness
Of this winter passage

Vivian Kearney

Montreal Winter

Snow falls amidst the purple
The rattle of a multi-colored train clatters
Rattles along toy mountains
It dances, it
Does all kinds of dances

Twinkling
Buildings
Smiles
Of a winter night

Seasonal

San Antonio in Winter

Twigs like rhyming runes
On the sidewalk
Shadow drawings
On the pavement

Windblown pebbles and leaves
Playing checkers with each other
Grasses sporting diamond drops
From yesterday's rains

Birds calling merrily
From feathery, frosty trees
Gently cool breezes
As we walk alongside
Cold black iron railings

All ask to be memorialized
When San Antonio's December
Is long gone

Vivian Kearney

Spring Power Points

Pale green leaves grow
Towards the peek-a-boo sun
Confused flowers bloom
Asking if the cold is done

Snow birds, feathered or not,
Think of flying home
Animals recently born
Wonder where they will roam

We pray to the
Hide and seek Lord
That the regreened earth
Be forever fully restored

Seasonal

Spring in San Antonio

The winter shivering branches
Of a neighboring mesquite
Are now draped with a delicate green lace shawl
Bluebonnets with their red, mauve
And yellow-hatted friends
Invite us to picnic with their light hearted companions
The dancing, frolicking, witty spring
Breezes

Vivian Kearney

Our Street Awakens

The newspaper isn't visible yet
Playing Easter egg hunt as always
Dawn beams through blue clouds
A brownish squirrel patters
Down a greyish tree trunk
A rose lends its bright smile
To this street's stories
On this miraculously average
Spring morning

Seasonal

Ice-Cream Summer

The pulsing liquid notes
Of the ice-cream truck's
Xylophone tunes
Drip through the thirsty
Summer air

Vivian Kearney

Summer in the Rio Grande Valley

Accumulating cumulus clouds
In a panoramic neon blue sky
Scrubbed by palms, mesquite and brush

Punctuated by exclamatory telephone poles
Contrasting with the few heat-laden trees
In the heart of the delta-veined, level
Rio Grande Valley

Seasonal

Watering the Sunset

Watering the sunset, pink and coral, grey and gold
Grass blades gladly wave their new pearl droplets
Pillowy clouds join to form partial continents
While the hose decides on its own mischievous dance

The partially dark houses, lawns reflect
Mysterious spots of light. All pray for rain
But the heavens are mum about this dry weather
Muttering — don't look to us, ask the Creator

Patterns of weeds show up in shadowy patches
My thoughts hop on multiple trains and buses
Insular dogs deem my routine not worth a warning
As the skies soft lullabies to the night city sing

Vivian Kearney

Whither the Weather

Vivian Kearney

Global Warming

Purple, yellow, red confetti
On the pearl-grey, sun-baked pavement
Of the second storey parking lot
Above the savory smells of the *mercado*

Which one will win in the end?
Will we have a paved earth
Overwhelmed by grey structures?

Or will the music, colors, cooking
Culture's celebrations
Reclaim our designs and visions
Like grasses through cement?

But global warming
Careless footprints
Might finally dry
All divergent plants

Northern Memories

Snow the sparkling,
Snow the freezing,
Snow for marveling,
Snow for playing

As cold stars
Adhere to
Our winterized skin

Night rainbows shimmering
Colorful curtains glowing
Dark skies transforming
Into virtual light shows

But we have to wonder
For how long?

Ice shelves dissolving
Ecologies disappearing...

As we are driven
By ever-grasping ads and habits
Our consuming toys
Aren't funny any more

Vivian Kearney

Drought - 2010

One little rumble
From on high
One darker cloud
In a pale blue sky

Two tiny raindrops
On the window pane
One haunted breeze
Swaying souls and leaves

In a celebration
Of long awaited rain

Drought - 2011

Little lost droplets
Sparkling on the night lawns
Sprinkler donated sparkles
Hinting to a dry sky
Still calm and lovely

It's time for the drought regions
To get some rain, end the pain
Of parched people, animals, plants
Bring back belated grasses, flowers
And even weeds again

Vivian Kearney

Dry News

The drought has exposed
Some human encampments
Perhaps predicting futures
For our present smug developments

Churches, graves, records, houses, implements
Revealed in dried lakes
Relate our histories again

What do they want to evidence this time
Is it a message, a prophecy, a portent or a sign
Is this weathered chance or a grand design
And what more will the next year find?

Drought - 2012

Why are we punished
By this lack of rain
Suffering nature's scorn
While fields are left forlorn

People of the Old Testament knew
But what can we pray or do
To regain God's grace
In this time and place

We witnessed blooms turned into deserts
Fruitful valleys dried and devastated
Flowers disappeared into sands and weeds
Grasses changed to stones by our greed

Maybe along with our ritualized pleas,
Enlisting wisdom long abandoned,
We can beg pardon and start again
And Creator and creation friendship mend

Vivian Kearney

Possible Sign - 2013

White rooster on the yellow grass
Of the fume-filled freeway median
Of course you're really made of paper
Only a poetizing creation

Pointing stalwartly to the north
Whence perhaps the rains might come
That this city so badly needs
Then your vigil will be done

Summer - 2014

Keep me entertained, retained
By beaded flashing rainbows
Virtual jewelled strands as I water
The lawn in this summer still too dry

Let each drop awaken a mentor
Angel for each plant to whisper —
Grow, grow, in spite of the drought
Under the hot San Antonio skies

Vivian Kearney

Torn the Feathers

Breakable the eggshells
Sharp the razor blades
Persuasive the myths
Scorned land without shade

But the clouds can carry
A cooling, forgiving rain
Transmitting our prayers
Granting an end to pain

Documentary - Sunken Paradise

Pacific islands going underwater —
Who will leave for a continental life
With problematic new starts, lost heritage?
And who will stay in this vanishing paradise?

Vivian Kearney

Concerns

This little earth swirled
In winds, cocooned
With clouds, marbled
White, blue, brown
And green

When will we handle it
Wholly, purely
In reasoned, heartfelt stewardship
Concerned
Not to let it fall

Tearing the Bonds

First
We crucified
Our Lord
Then
We crucified
The world
He made

Vivian Kearney

Save Us (Hoshianu)

Vivian Kearney

Across Time

Maybe when they find the
Higgs-Boson particle and then
Hold it under an electron-microscope
They'll see therein
A tiny garden
With a miniscule Adam and Eve
Newly created
Full of joy and hope

And we'll try to warn them
And ourselves to walk with love
To live wisely with God's gifts of grace

But who will teach us their language?
Can we read each other's faces?

Two steps back
Maybe two and a half
Forward to the future.

Lord, if we can't reach our ancestors
Help us speak to our descendants
This world's new cast

Save Us (*Hoshianu*)

Lost

Lost dog's picture
On a lost torn poster
Where are you wandering?
Do you know your way home?

Lost nations warring
On a polluted lost planet
What will become of you?
Where is humanity's home?

Vivian Kearney

They Will Start to Sing

Suddenly
In church
The wall-lining stones
Rough-hewn and pockmarked
Signalled...

We were there, maybe
At the beginning
With the worshipping
First followers

Put us together
And we can form a choir
Gathering with the tensile
Story-telling glass
Warm wood
Witnessing lights
Resonating crosses

Remembering,
Echoing our cousins
Who sang for
Jesus

Save Us (*Hoshianu*)

Holy Ground

Let's
Take the risk to
Walk slowly
Into a worshipful
Spiritual place

And breathe with our souls,
Look with our hearts
At the cathedral clouds
Listen with our spirits
To the symphonies in the wind

Then
Let's write what they tell us
About God, the Creator
The Musician, the Architect, the Artist,
The Messiah, the Savior,
The Comforter

Vivian Kearney

Wellsprings Chapel

Tiny stars of white weed flowers
By puzzle pieces of grey
Flagstones leading inside
To the outside

Windows mirroring
Candles in the clouds
Chandeliers in the skies

Nest on an outside crossbeam
Brown bird on fence
Momentarily listening
Faithful trees swaying
To hymns over blue-green hills

Beyond the glass
Giant striding
Statue of Jesus
His arms outstretched
Like the embracing waking fields
His face like that of His shroud

Far away red-roofed civilization
Near windows of salvation

Nature one with us
Jesus one with us

Save Us (*Hoshianu*)

At the Bench

Whom should we thank
O whom should we praise
For a firefly of an airplane buzzing through the skies
Under a white sail of a moon
Through purple watercolor clouds
Black green silhouettes of leaves
Preening their surreal ties

Wonders of twilights, symphonies of dawns
Urging us to join in their meditative songs
Cheery campfires of lamps, some moving, some still
Declare that to the Creator we all finally belong

We are part of His painting, figures in His plan,
Threads in His mantle, notes in His tunes
And through beauty's truths, truth's beauties
Our oceanic hearts are moved by His good news

Vivian Kearney

Prismatic

A hello of yellow,
A sigh of blue,
A hope of green,
A smile of orange,
A touch of mauve,
A meditation of purple,
A wonder of gold,
A proclamation of red —

God loves you
Is what
The rainbow
Said

www.ingramcontent.com/pod-product-compliance
Lightning Source LLC
Chambersburg PA
CBHW032141040426
42449CB00005B/341